SMART BRAIN RIGHT BRAIN

An Introduction to Electrical Engineering

Om KIDZ
An imprint of Om Books International

First Published in 2021 by

Om Kidz | Om Books International

Corporate & Editorial Office
A-12, Sector 64, Noida 201 301
Uttar Pradesh, India
Phone: +91 120 477 4100
Email: editorial@ombooks.com
Website: www.ombooksinternational.com

Sales Office
107, Ansari Road, Darya Ganj
New Delhi 110 002, India
Phone: +91 11 4000 9000
Email: sales@ombooks.com

Author: Shweta Sinha
Editor: Kirti Pathak
Art & Design: Anshuman Pandey, Gaurav Bhandari, Harish Arya

ISBN: 978-93-5276-844-8

Printed in India

10 9 8 7 6 5 4 3 2 1

CONTENTS

1. What Is Engineering?

Engineering is finding solutions to human needs. Engineers are people who design, build and test new and useful things that make our lives better. Engineers use science and mathematics to help make almost everything we use—from cars to a toothbrush.

The engineering process

1. Ask

What is the problem that needs a solution?

I need a faster bicycle to ride to school.

2. Imagine

How to solve the problem? Brainstorm and research solutions.

3. Plan

How will the solution look like? Make detailed designs.

4. Create

Let's build! Create a model of the solution and test how well it works.

5. Improve

Keep working on the design to make it better and better. Test and share the final design.

The engineering process does not end with building a final working model. Engineers keep thinking of new ways to improve the design and make things better.

POCKET FACT

Engineers usually don't work alone. A team of engineers work together when they plan, design, build and test products.

What do Electrical Engineers do?

Can you spot the devices in this house that run on electricity?

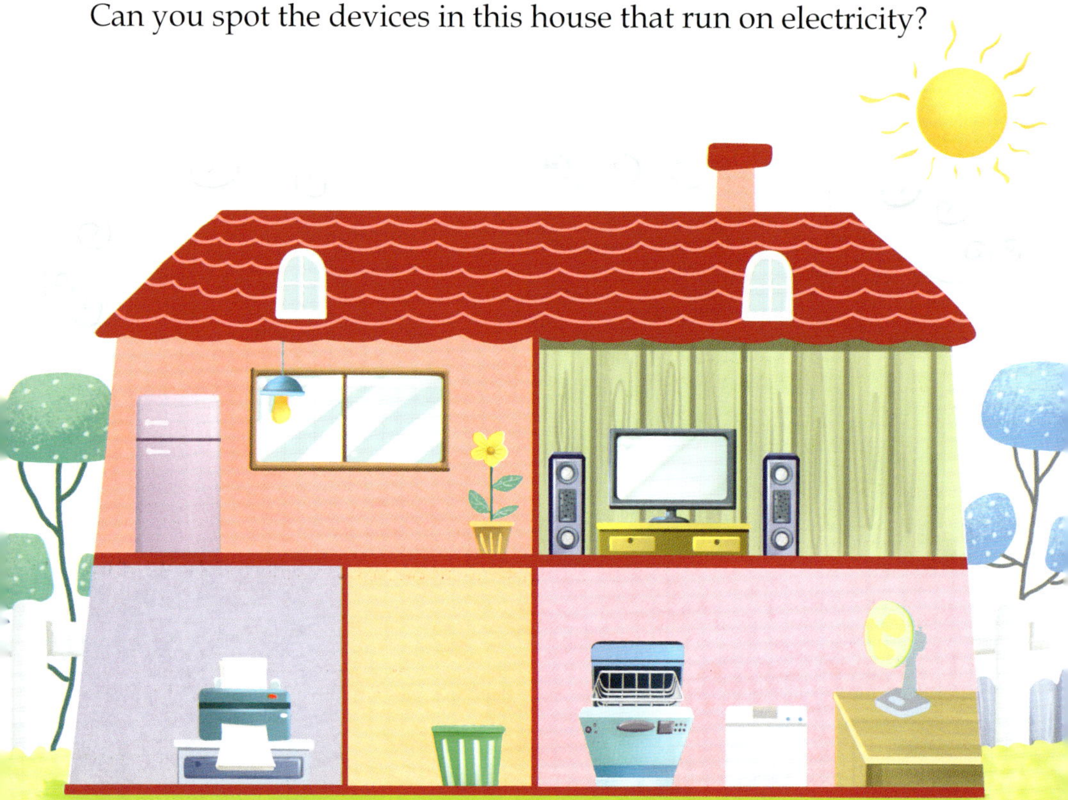

What electrical devices do you use at home? Do you enjoy watching cartoons on television? Perhaps you play video games with your friends. The air conditioning keeps your house cool during summers. When you feel hungry, you heat up a bag of popcorn in the microwave. The refrigerator keeps the ice-cream frozen. Even the computer is rarely shut down.

Have you noticed that all these devices are connected to an electrical socket on the wall? They all run on electricity. Some devices are also powered by batteries. The TV remote control is one such battery-powered electrical device. Electrical engineers help make all the electrical devices you can think of. They design, create, build, test and fix machines that use electricity.

POCKET FACT Devices that run on electricity are called electrical devices.

Some electrical engineers work on the generation of electricity. Some others help improve the network that delivers electricity to homes and schools. Yet others design the electrical systems inside devices or may specialise in medical equipments. Without electrical engineers, even computers would not have been built.

2. What Is Electricity?

Electricity is a type of energy. It is the flow of electric charge. You must have seen mighty lightning bolts tearing through the sky during a thunderstorm. A lightning bolt is a flow of electric charge in nature.

Static vs. Current Electricity

Have you felt a little zap when you touched something metal, like a door handle? This is an example of **static electricity**. Static electricity gathers and stays in one place.

When electricity flows from one place to another, it becomes **current electricity**. We get an electric current in our homes to run our electrical devices.

Electricity and Conductors

Current electricity needs a medium to flow through. Materials that allow electricity to flow easily are called **good conductors**. Many metals are good conductors. Electrical engineers use such good conductors in their designs.

Inside all electrical cables are metal wires that conduct electricity. The most common metals used to make wires are copper and aluminium.

DID YOU KNOW? Gold and silver are also good conductors of electricity, but are not commonly used as they are expensive.

Who discovered Electricity?

Electricity has always been present in nature in many forms. An electric eel produces electricity in its body. It can give a shock big enough to hurt a horse. A bolt of lightning occurs when an enormous amount of static electricity builds up in the clouds. Our bodies have electricity too. It helps our heart to beat.

The History of Electricity

About 200 years ago, people did not know much about electricity. There were no light bulbs or any of the electrical devices we use today. A scientist called Benjamin Franklin was quite intrigued by lightning bolts. He believed that a lightning bolt was nothing but electricity.

One day, there was a big thunderstorm where he lived. Benjamin took out a kite, tied a metal key on the string and flew the kite into the storm. Sparks from the clouds flowed through the string and into the metal key. The experiment was extremely dangerous. It could have killed Benjamin, but he was able to prove to the world that a lightning bolt indeed was electricity.

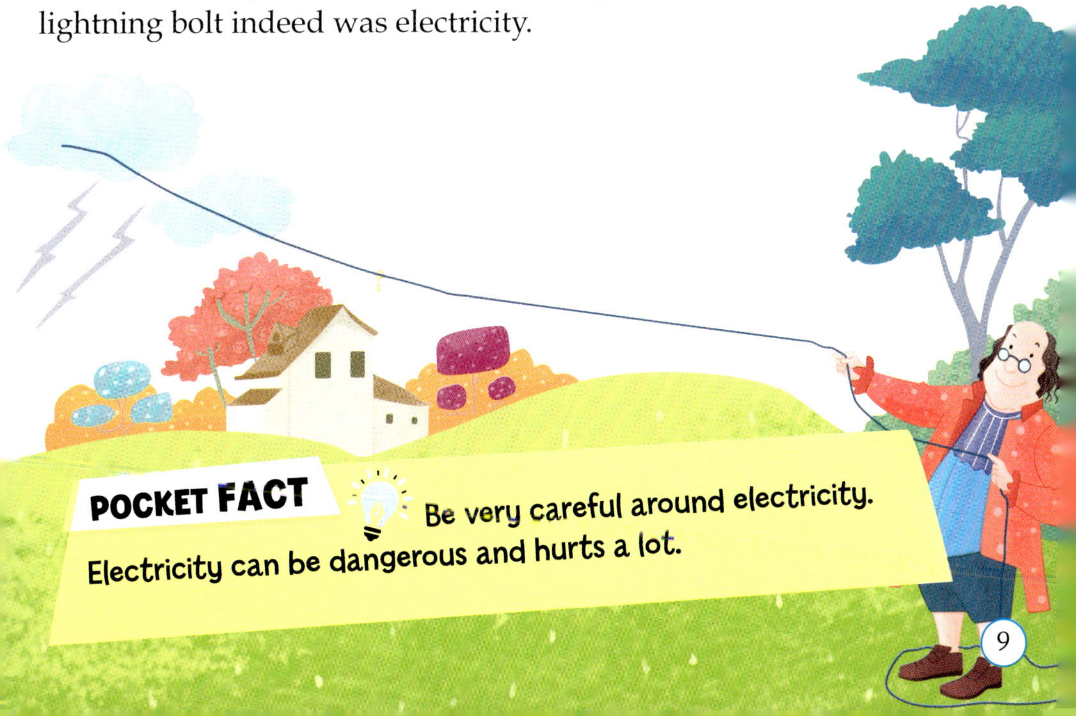

POCKET FACT Be very careful around electricity. Electricity can be dangerous and hurts a lot.

3. Electrical Circuit

An electrical circuit is a path around which electricity moves. All electrical devices have a circuit inside them. Closing this path lets the electric current flow and switches on the device. Opening or breaking the circuit switches off the device.

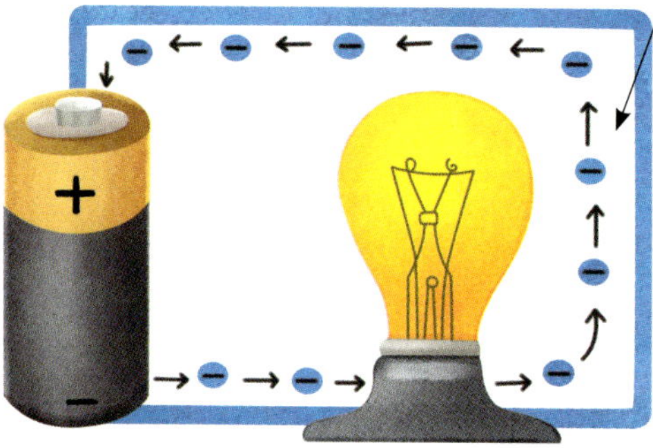

Closed Circuit

Electricity moving along a closed circuit

Open Circuit

Electricity cannot flow if there is a break or gap in the circuit.

We use a switch to turn on or turn off electrical devices. A switch breaks the circuit and stops the flow of electricity. This is why a switch is also known as a circuit breaker.

POCKET FACT

Materials that make it difficult for electricity to flow through them are called insulators. Rubber and plastic are insulators.

You can make a circuit by connecting electrical components with a wire. A circuit must have an electricity source to work.

A **torch** or a **flashlight** is a portable electrical device used to give light. A simple circuit inside a flashlight consists of batteries, one or more bulbs and a switch, all linked by wires.

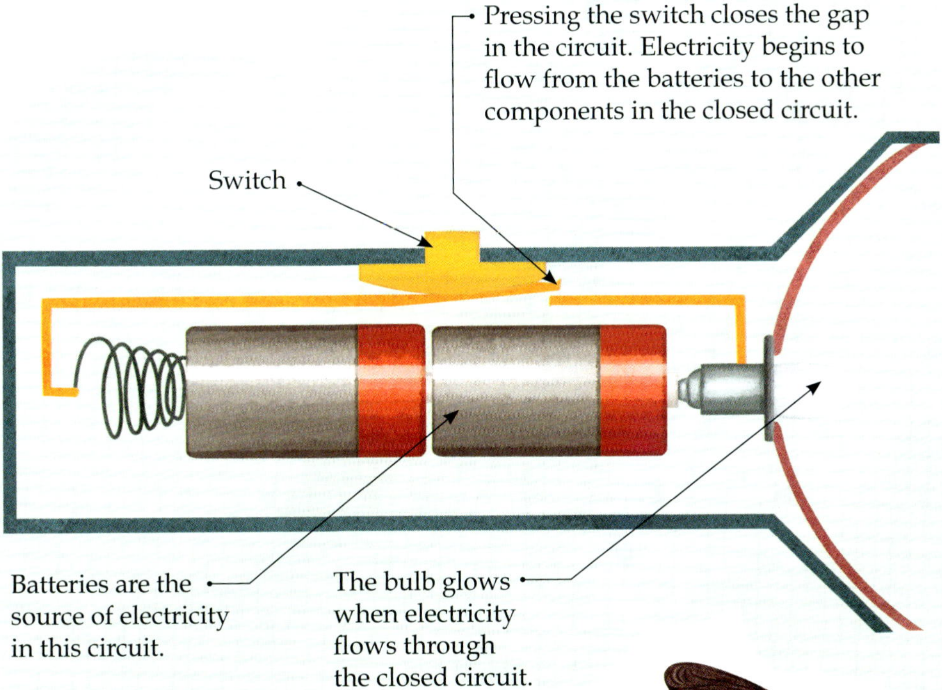

DID YOU KNOW?

When a lightning bolt falls on Earth from the sky, a circuit is formed by the air between the ground and the storm cloud.

4. Making Electricity

You flip on a switch and the bulb lights up or the computer starts working. Electricity is always there when you need it. While some houses are equipped to generate their own electricity, most often this is not the case. Electricity travels many miles from a generating station through cables and wires to reach your home.

Power Plants

A power plant or a generating station is a place where electricity is produced. A majority of power plants use massive machines called turbines and generators to make electricity.

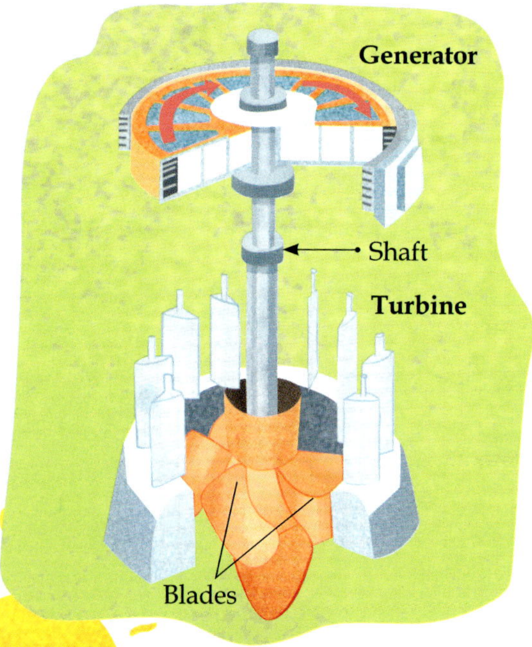

A **turbine** is a large wheel with blades like a windmill. The turbine is connected to a **generator**. When the turbine spins, the generator produces electricity. A power plant just needs to keep spinning the turbine to generate electricity.

In a typical power plant, the power of steam is used to turn the turbine. Tons of water is boiled to generate huge amounts of steam. Fossil fuel, such as coal, is burned in order to boil water.

DID YOU KNOW?

Wind, solar and water are some of the other sources of energy used by power plants to generate electricity.

Hydroelectricity

A hydroelectric power plant uses the force of moving water to turn the turbine. Hydroelectric power plants are built near big rivers, where they use the movement of water in two ways:

1. The natural flow of the river.

2. The force of water falling down. For this, a dam is created on the river, letting the water fill a reservoir or a lake. A dam is a manmade structure with gates. The gates let go a portion of the water from the lake into the river at the bottom, making the water fall down.

The flowing or falling water is forced through a pipe called a penstock. This force pushes the blades of the turbine and makes it spin.

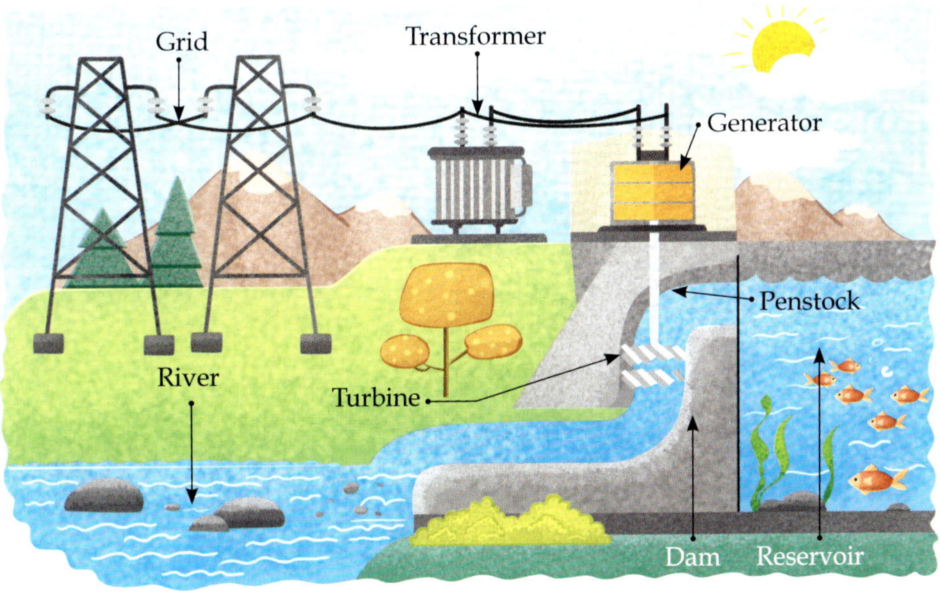

POCKET FACT

A tidal power plant makes use of the daily rise and fall of tides in oceans and seas to generate electricity.

Moving Electricity

You might have noticed huge towers with power lines suspended between them along highways. Or perhaps, there are poles on the street outside your house. Those power lines running from tower to tower and pole to pole connect the power plants to all the houses, offices and schools that need electricity. Here is how electricity reaches us:

1. Electricity is generated in a power plant. Power plants are usually located in remote areas, far from human settlements.

2. Huge transformers increase the voltage of electricity. High voltage helps electricity travel long distances.

3. High voltage transmission lines running between metal towers carry electricity all across the country. The metal towers or pylons are built to be quite tall in order to keep the transmission lines high above the ground.

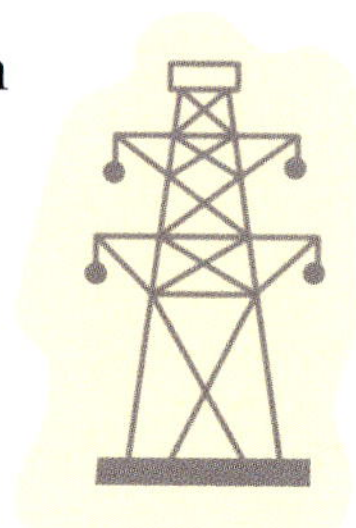

4. Closer to its destination, a substation lowers the voltage of electricity. Only then the current is sent over smaller power lines.

DID YOU KNOW?

Even the power plants across the country are connected to each other. This network is known as the power grid.

5. A network of distribution lines connect a sub-station to the buildings in the area. Most distribution lines run safely underground. In some places, they also run from pole to pole along the streets. The voltage is further lowered by smaller transformers on poles or on the ground before supplying the current to homes. A lower voltage makes electricity safe for our use.

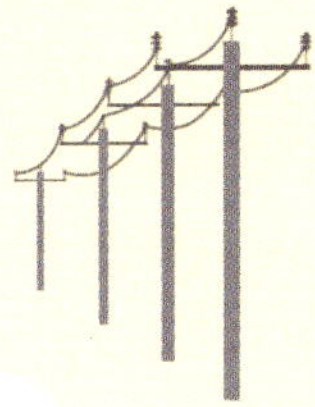

6. A meter at every home keeps track of the amount of electricity used there. We need to pay the government to use electricity from the power grid.

7. The electric current flows through a breaker box before getting distributed around the house. The box has fuses and breakers that keep the house safe from any overloading inside the house.

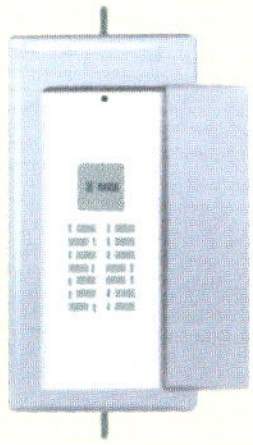

8. Inside our homes, wires usually run inside the walls, carrying electricity to all the power outlets and switches.

POCKET FACT

'Voltage' is a measure of the force that electricity applies when it moves through a conductor.

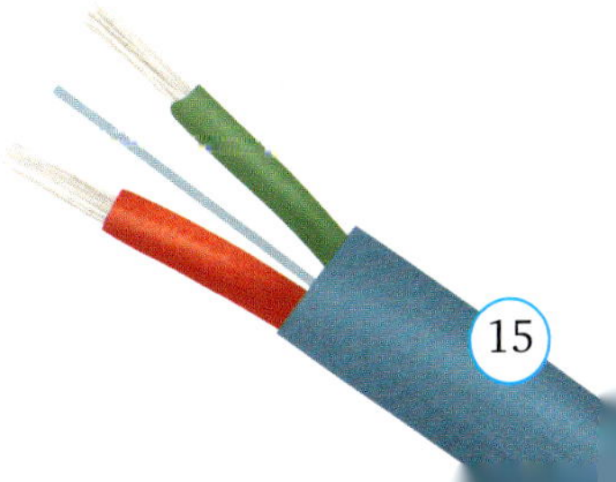

5. Electricity from Sunlight

Some houses are able to generate their own electricity. Solar panels installed on their rooftops use the power of the Sun to make electricity.

Solar Energy

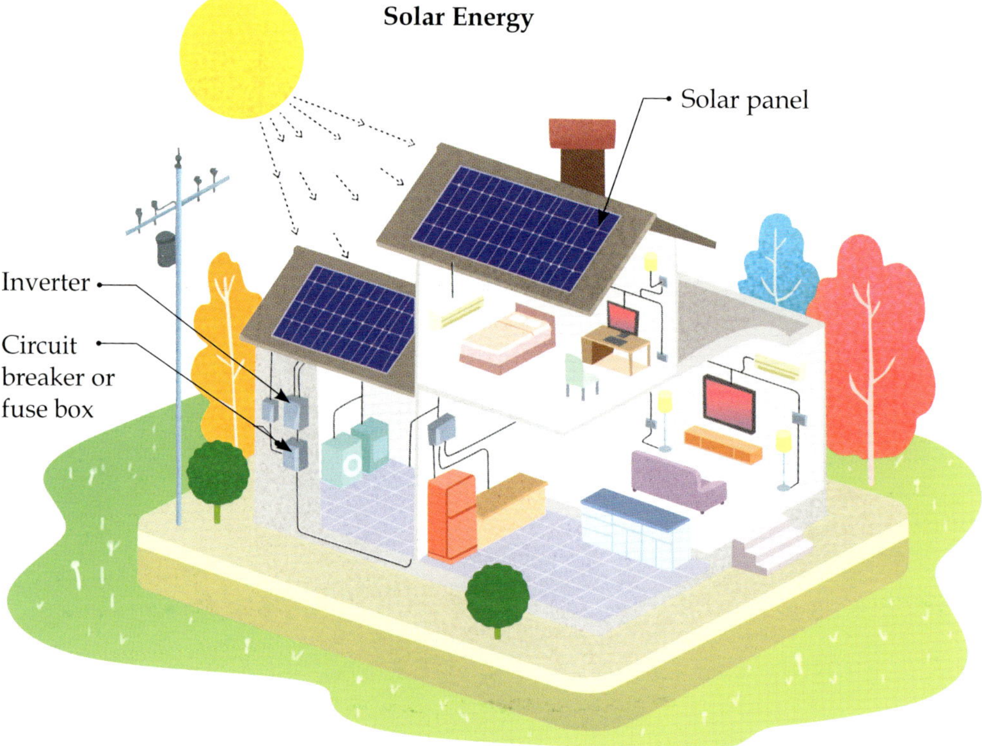

The solar panels capture the sunlight and create electricity. This electricity is fed into an inverter. The inverter converts it into an electric current suitable for electrical devices. The current then passes through the breaker box before getting distributed around the house.

POCKET FACT

Since solar panels cannot work at night, the house still needs to be connected to the electricity supply from the power grid.

How do solar panels work?

A solar panel is like a sandwich with many layers. A metal frame gives structure and support to the panel. A layer of photovoltaic solar cells is the most important layer. These solar cells are made from a non-metal called silicon. A layer of glass casing protects the solar cells from weather and airborne particles. In addition, various wiring inside the solar panel connect the solar cells to the inverter inside the house.

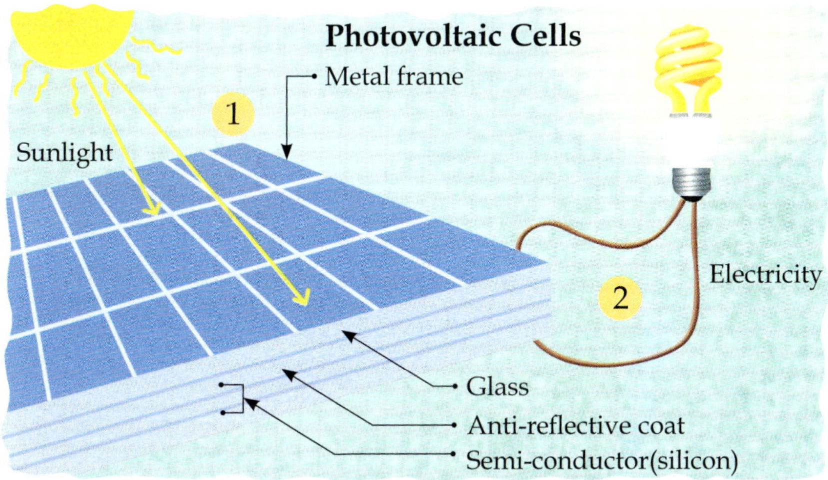

Here is how electricity is made by a solar panel:

1. The solar cells absorb sunlight. When the Sun's rays interact with the silicon in the solar cells, it creates a flow of electric current.
2. Wires in the panels capture and carry out the electricity and lead it to the inverter for further distribution.

DID YOU KNOW?

Any unused electricity generated by the solar panels can be fed back into the power grid. The government pays the house owner for the same.

6. Battery

Several electrical devices run on batteries. Batteries are portable sources of electricity. You may have seen batteries inside toys, a torch or a wall clock.

Batteries come in many shapes and sizes.

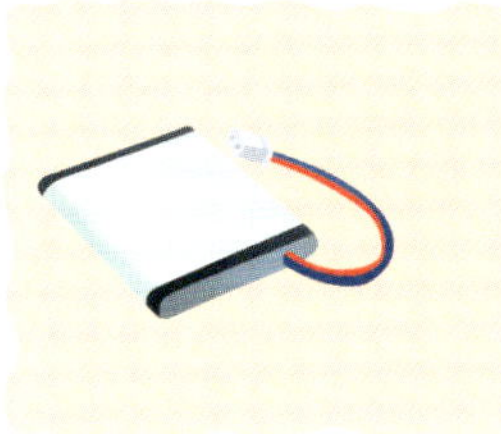

A mobile phone has a rechargeable **ion-lithium battery**. It is usually safely hidden inside and you don't get to see it often.

A car has a battery under its hood. The car battery is much heavier and bigger in size.

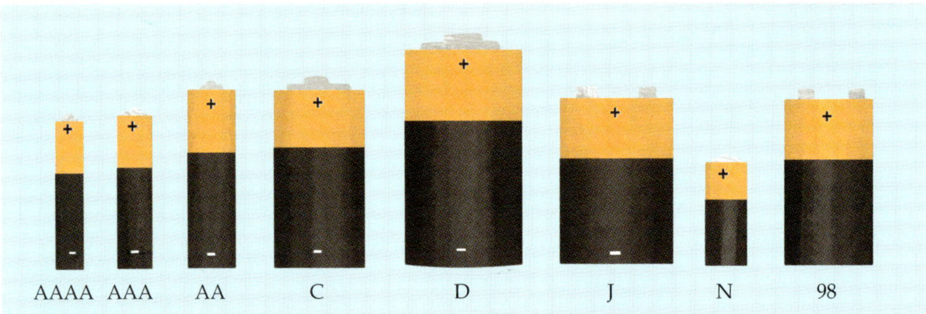

However, the mostly commonly used batteries are the **dry cell batteries**. They too come in a variety of shapes and sizes. The amount of electric charge a battery can supply depends on the size of the battery. Typically, bigger batteries provide more electric charge.

DID YOU KNOW? You can make a battery from citrus fruits like lemons. They have a chemical called citric acid that can generate small amounts of power.

How does a battery work?

A battery makes electricity with the reaction of certain chemicals. It uses the energy stored inside the chemicals to push out an electric current into the circuit. The outer jacket of a battery is made of an insulating material so it is safe for us to handle. A battery has a positive end, marked with a '+' sign and a negative end marked with a '-' sign. In between the two lies a chemical paste known as electrolyte.

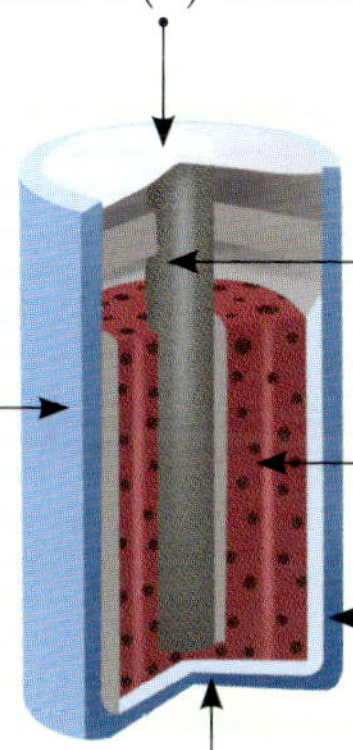

Chemical reactions take place in the electrolyte, resulting in an electric current. The two electrodes allow electricity to pass through. Electric current from a battery always flows in a fixed direction in the circuit. The current is pushed out from the battery's negative end into the circuit and goes back into the battery at the positive end.

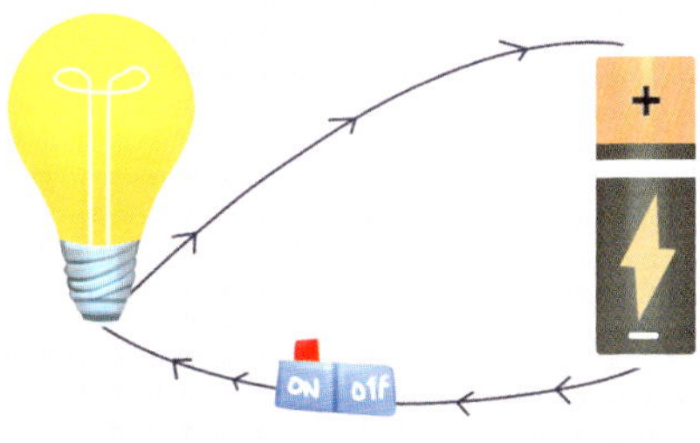

POCKET FACT

A battery is called a wet or dry cell battery depending on the type of electrolyte it holds. A car battery is a wet cell battery as it contains a liquid.

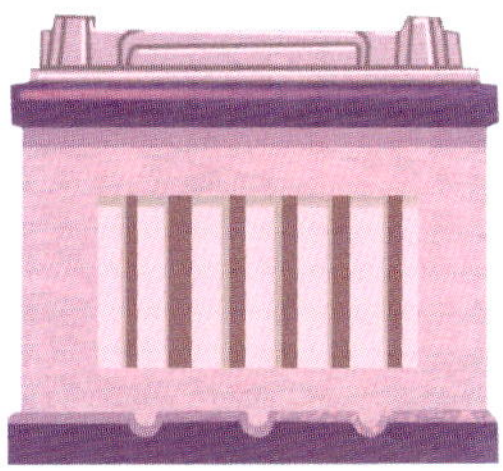

7. Using Electricity

Since the time electricity became available, engineers have been thinking up new uses for it . Today, it is difficult to imagine our lives without electricity. Electricity has a lot of power. It can run the fastest trains in the world. At the same time, electricity also powers the smallest of gadgets like a mobile phone.

Let there be light

The **light bulb** was invented in the 19th century. However, the early light bulbs were not very practical. It was Thomas Edison, an American scientist and inventor, who improved upon the light bulb. His design made the bulb shine brighter and last longer. It was also more affordable. Soon people began replacing candles and oil lamps with light bulbs in their homes. Today, a light bulb is one of the most widely used electrical appliances.

DID YOU KNOW?

Before electricity, fireplaces kept homes warm, oil lamps and candles gave light and food was kept cool in iceboxes or underground storage cellars.

An **incandescent light bulb** works by sending an electric current through a thin wire called a filament. The filament begins to glow, producing light.

The modern **fluorescent light bulb** works in a slightly different manner. Instead of a filament, it holds a mix of gases inside a tube. When an electric current is passed through it, an invisible ultraviolet (UV) light is created. The white coating converts this UV light into a bright white light.

An **LED** (Light Emitting Diode) bulb gives off a lot of light with very little electricity. They work with an electronic microchip made from silicon.

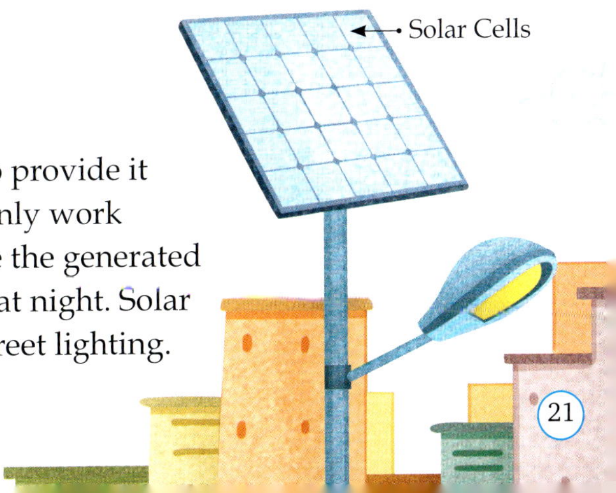

A **solar lamp** has solar cells to provide it with electricity. Solar lamps only work outside. They are able to store the generated electricity in batteries for use at night. Solar lamps are typically used in street lighting.

Turning Electricity into Heat

Electricity and heat are both forms of energy. When electricity flows through a wire, some of the electrical energy gets converted into heat and makes the wire hot. This property is used by many heating appliances.

A **water kettle** has a coil that heats up when electricity is passed through it. The heated coil heats the water in turn. However, water is a good conductor of electricity. A combination of the two can be deadly. Hence, the coil has to be kept separated from the water. The earlier electric kettles kept the coil at a distance from the water. However, that led to a lot of the heat getting lost in the air. In modern kettles, the coil is safely encased inside waterproof insulators.

An electric water heater or a **geyser** is used to provide hot water directly into a tap. Unlike a kettle, a geyser needs to heat up a large quantity of water at a time. However, both devices work in the same manner. A geyser too has well-insulated heating coils inside it that are connected to an electricity source by wires. When current passes through it, it heats the coil. The heated coil then heats up the water.

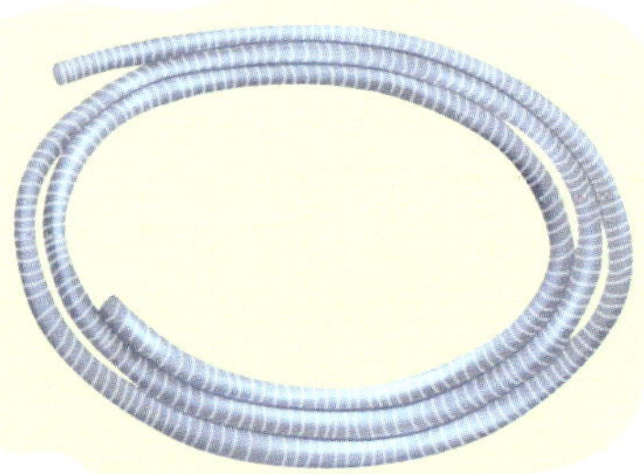

POCKET FACT

Heating coils are made of metals that give some resistance to the electric current. The resistance makes them get heated.

An **electric iron** has a coil inside it too. When you turn on the appliance, the coil gets heated. The heat is then transferred to the metallic base plate. When you press the iron against your clothes, the heat smoothens out the wrinkles and creases.

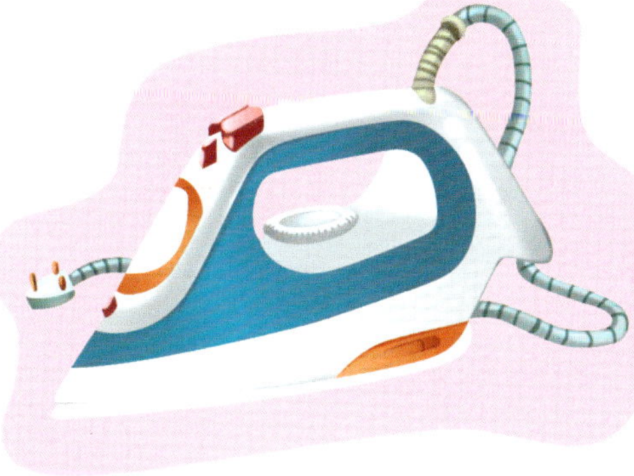

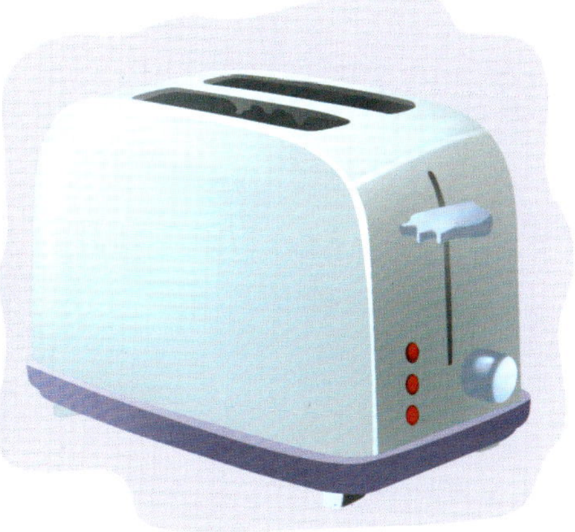

If you look inside a **toaster**, you will notice its thin, bare metal coils turn red hot when you switch on the toaster. A toaster often has a timer or a thermostat to switch off the device when the bread is done. A timer is based on a specific period of time, while a thermostat keeps track of the temperature.

An **electric oven** is used to bake bread and cook many kinds of your favourite dishes. Inside the oven are large coils of wire called heating elements. A thermostat keeps the temperature inside the oven constant so the food does not burn.

DID YOU KNOW?

A toaster may be small compared to an oven, but it consumes half as much electricity as the oven.

Electricity and Motion

An **electric motor** converts electrical energy into mechanical energy or motion.

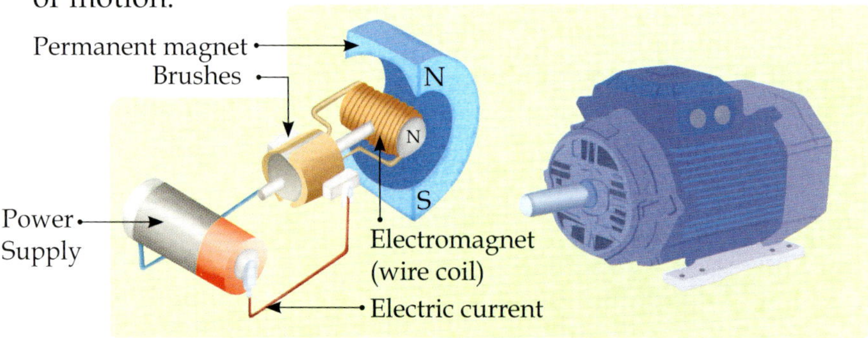

A motor has an electric supply, a permanent magnet and an electromagnet that can rotate. When electricity flows through the coil of the electromagnet, it creates a magnetic field around the coil. This magnetic field interacts with the magnetic field of the permanent magnet and causes the electromagnet to rotate. We use many appliances that use this motion to perform a mechanical task.

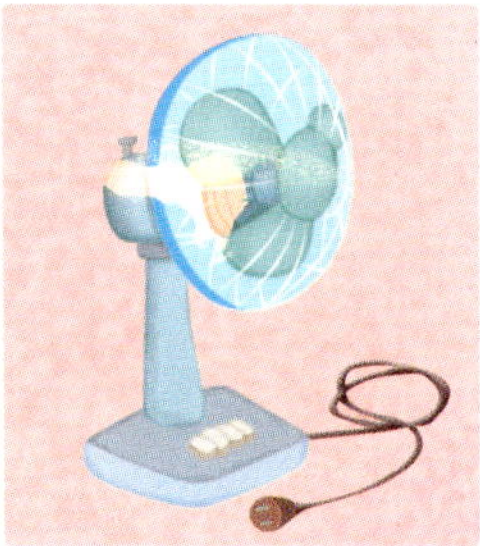

An electric motor inside a fan makes its blades spin. As the blades spin, it creates movement in the air that cools us on a hot day.

Washing machines, dishwashers, drills and blenders are all appliances that have an electric motor that converts electrical energy into mechanical energy.

POCKET FACT

Electric motors vary in size from small, battery-powered ones for toys to bigger ones that drive trains and trams.

Turning Electricity into Sound

A **speaker** is a device that takes in an electric signal and converts it into a sound. Without a speaker, we would not have any audio in our televisions. The radio would not work. Even computers, telephones and the tiniest of ear bud headphones have speakers inside them.

Parts of a Speaker

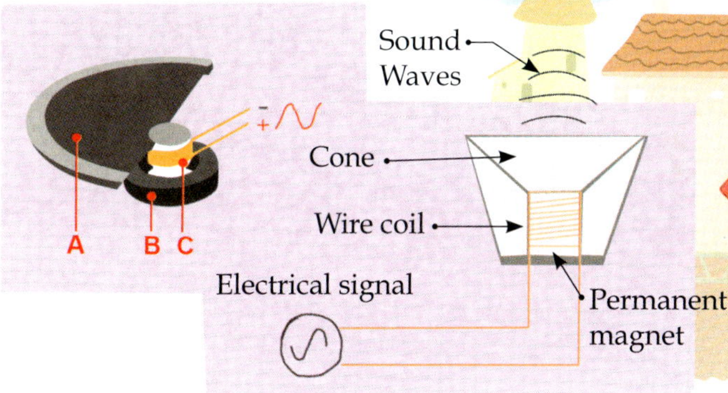

A. **Cone** - This is the part that moves and produces a sound.

B. **Permanent Magnet**

C. **Voice Coil or Wire Coil**

Like in a motor, the electric current produces a magnetic field around the coil. This interacts with the magnetic field of the permanent magnet, making the coil move up and down. As the coil moves, it pulls and pushes the cone. The back and forth movement of the cone pumps out sounds in the air. So, a speaker first converts electric energy into mechanical energy, which is then converted into sound energy.

DID YOU KNOW?

A microphone functions opposite to a speaker. It takes in sound energy and converts it into electric signals.

8. Activity: Let's make a circuit

Build a simple circuit to make a light bulb glow. **Take a grownup's help** for this activity.

You need:

- Cardboard from a cereal box
- Aluminium foil
- 2 binder clips and paper clips
- 2 AA batteries and a battery holder
- An LED bulb
- Scissors, tape

Step 1. Cut a rectangular strip with the cardboard, about 1.5 inches wide and 3 inches long.

Step 2. Cut out two strips of aluminium foil, each 1 inch wide and 3 inches long.

Step 3. Wrap the aluminium strips along the long edges of the cardboard. Secure them with tape. This makes your circuit board.

Step 4. Gently bend the legs of the LED and connect it to the circuit board. Make sure each leg touches the aluminium foil.

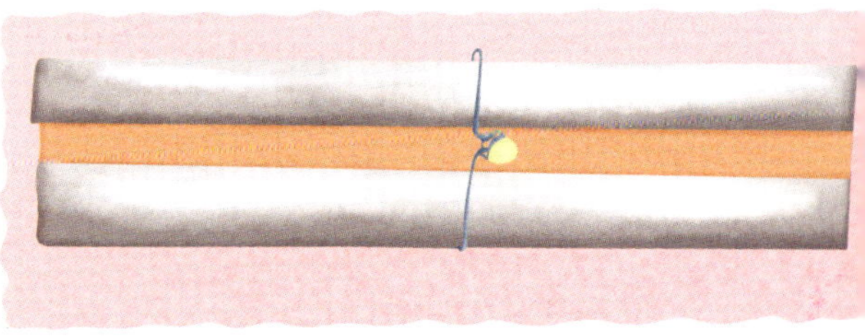

Step 5. Notice that the legs are not the same length. The longer leg connects to the positive (+) side of the battery. Mark the sides of the circuit board with a '+' symbol on the side that has the longer leg and a '-' on the other side. Use the binder clips to hold the legs to the foil.

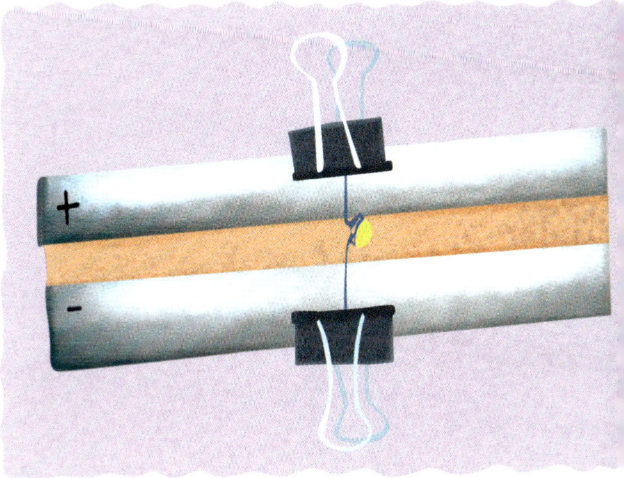

Step 6. Connect the two AA batteries to the circuit board. Hold the end of the red wire from the positive (+) side of the battery to the positive (+) foil strip with a paper clip.

Step 7. Carefully touch the black wire to the negative (-) foil strip. You should see the LED glow. Remove the black wire and the bulb stops glowing.

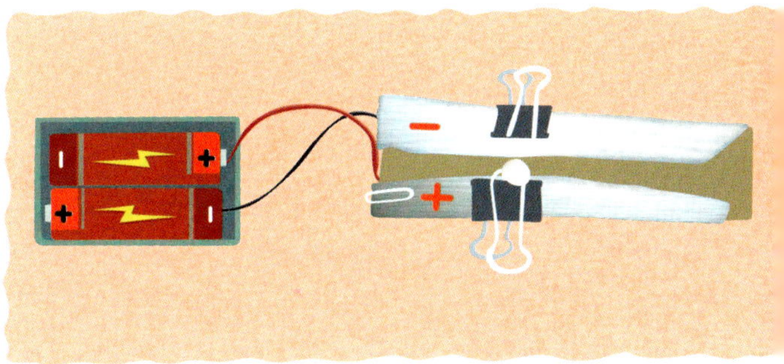

What happened?

When you touch the black wire to the foil, it creates a closed circuit. Electricity begins to flow and makes the LED glow. When you remove the black wire, it breaks or opens the circuit.

Try this:

Touch the black wire to the cardboard. Will the bulb glow?

Answer: The bulb will not glow. The cardboard is an insulator and does not let electricity to pass through.

Let's Get Active

Crossword Puzzle

Fill in the crossword puzzle by answering the questions in the clues given below.

Across

6. A device that increases or reduces the voltage of electricity.

7. At a power plant, this massive machine is kept spinning to generate electricity.

10. These people design, build and test new and useful things that make our lives better.

11. An incomplete path that does not allow electric current to flow.

12. This non-metal is used in solar cells.

Down

1. A material that allows the flow of electricity.

2. Electricity and heat, both are types of this.

3. A portable source of electricity.

4. A complete path allowing electric current to flow.

5. This type of light bulb has a thin wire called a filament.

8. A material that slows the flow of energy.

9. A kettle, toaster and an iron convert electrical energy into this form of energy.

12. Solar panels make electricity from the energy of the ____.

The Journey of Electricity

How does electricity reach your home? Number the steps in the correct order:

Electricity generation

1

Distribution

Using electricity

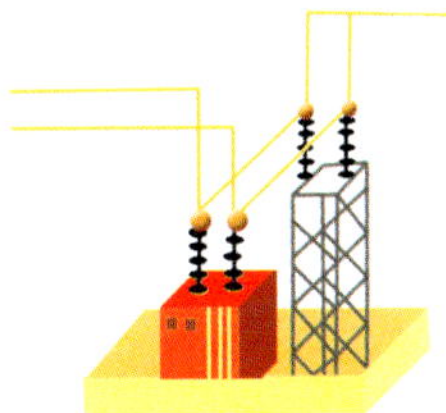

Voltage increase

Transmission along power lines

Substation reduces voltage

Test your knowledge

Choose the best option to complete the sentence.

1. Copper and aluminium are ___________ .

   (a) conductors

   (b) insulators

   (c) semi-conductors

2. Power plants make electricity using two massive machines, _______ and ______.

   (a) windmill, transformer

   (b) transformer, generator

   (c) turbine, generator

3. A ______ is used to increase as well as decrease the voltage of electricity.

   (a) turbine

   (b) transformer

   (c) transmitter

4. A battery is filled with a mix of chemicals called the __________.

   (a) electrode

   (b) terminal

   (c) electrolyte

5. A device that drives all these machines - a toy car, a bullet train, a fan and a washing machine.

   (a) electric motor

   (b) electromagnet

   (c) heating coil

6. A speaker converts the electrical energy first into _______ energy and then into ______ energy.

   (a) sound, heat

   (b) mechanical, sound

   (c) sound, mechanical

Close the Circuit

Nigel wants to listen to some music, but all his wires from the power source have got entangled. Help him connect all his wires correctly to close the circuit, so he can turn on the music.

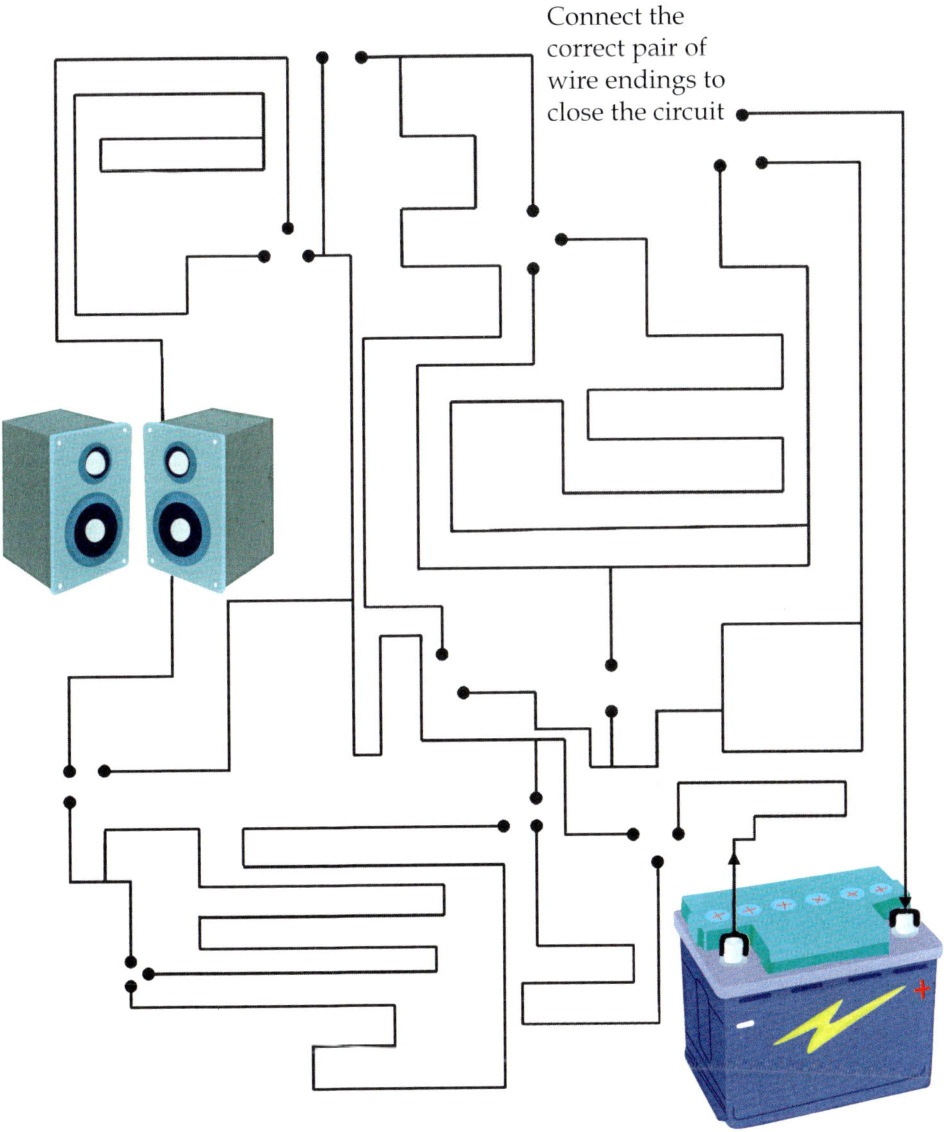

GLOSSARY

Chemical	a substance that cannot be broken down without changing it into something else, e.g. water and oxygen
Electromagnet	an electromagnet is a magnet that runs on electricity
Experiment	a scientific procedure undertaken to make a discovery
Fuse	a safety device that breaks an electric circuit if the current exceeds a safe level
Gadget	a small mechanical or electronic device or tool
Mechanical	relating to physical forces or motion
Microphone	an instrument for converting sound waves into electrical energy
Non-metal	an element or substance that is not a metal
Portable	something that is small and portable
Reaction	a chemical process in which substances act mutually on each other and are changed into different substances
Remote	situated far from the main centres of population
Reservoir	a large natural or artificial lake
Resistance	the use of force to oppose something
Settlement	a place where people establish a community
Solution	products or services designed to meet a particular need
Ultraviolet	a type of rays or waves of light

ANSWERS

Page 28.

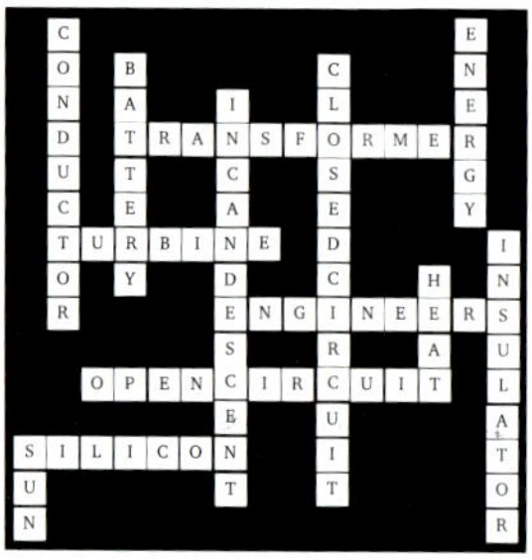

Page 29.

1. Electricity generation
2. Voltage increase
3. Transmission along power lines
4. Substation reduces voltage
5. Distribution
6. Using electricity

Page 30. 1.(a); 2.(c); 3.(b)

4.(c); 5.(a); 6.(b)

Page 31.

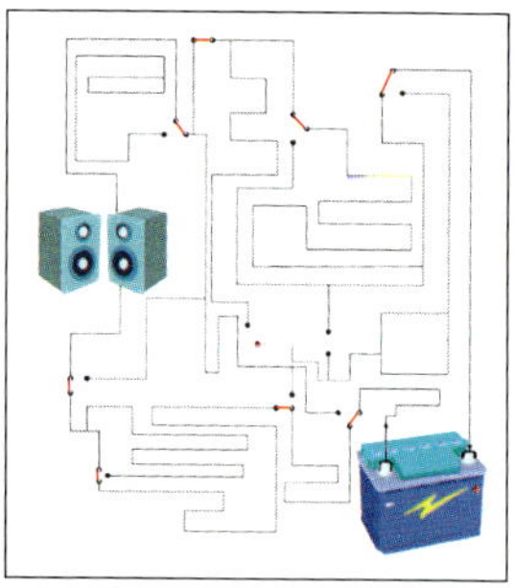